I0006328

AH! WHY AI KEEPS MAKING THINGS UP

Alfonso Borello

Villaggio Publishing Ltd

Cover design by Alfonso Borello
Printed in the United States of America

CONTENTS

PREFACE

The desire to understand and replicate human intelligence has a long and winding road. From the early ponderings of ancient philosophers like Aristotle and Plato to the ingenious automatons of Hero of Alexandria and Leonardo da Vinci, the seeds of artificial intelligence (AI) were sown long ago. These early creations sparked the question: could machines ever truly think?

The formalization of logic systems in the 19th century provided a crucial springboard. By capturing the essence of reasoning and problem-solving in a structured way, these systems offered a blueprint for replicating intelligence in machines. The mid-20th century marked a turning point. The advent of powerful computers allowed scientists like Alan Turing, with his Turing Test, and John McCarthy, who coined the term itself, to truly launch the field of AI research. Their focus? Programming machines to perform tasks that required intelligence.

The motivations behind AI research are as complex as the field itself. At its core lies the fundamental question of whether machines can ever truly mimic human thought and reason. Beyond that, there's a deep-seated human desire to automate tasks, particularly those that are repetitive, mundane, or even dangerous. AI offers the potential to free us from such burdens.

Also, AI systems hold immense potential for problem-solving and decision-making. Their ability to analyze vast amounts of data and identify patterns invisible to humans makes them invaluable tools in fields like medicine, finance, and scientific research. Ultimately, AI isn't just about replicating intelligence; it's about augmenting our own capabilities. By assisting us in making better decisions, enhancing our creativity, and pushing the boundaries of discovery, AI has the potential to usher in a new era of human achievement.

As we explore the ever-expanding potential of AI, understanding its origins and motivations is paramount. It allows us to navigate the ethical considerations that come with such powerful technology and ensure it benefits humanity for generations to come.

Layers of Interpretations: AI Through Different Lenses

Artificial intelligence (AI) sparks a range of interpretations, depending on your perspective. Here's a glimpse into how different groups view this evolving technology:

The Skeptics: Some remain unconvinced, questioning whether AI can ever truly achieve human-level intelligence. They might point to the limitations of current AI systems, highlighting their inability to replicate the full spectrum of human thought, creativity, and social intelligence.

The Believers: Enthusiasts, on the other hand, envision a future where AI surpasses human limitations. They see AI as a powerful tool for solving complex problems, from eradicating diseases to tackling climate change. They believe AI has the potential to revolutionize virtually every aspect of our lives.

The Bureaucrats: Caught in the middle are policymakers and regulators. They grapple with the ethical considerations surrounding AI, such as bias in algorithms and the potential for job displacement due to automation. They seek clear answers about the responsible development and deployment of AI to ensure it benefits society without unintended consequences.

Understanding these diverse viewpoints is crucial for navigating the future of AI. Skepticism keeps us grounded, ensuring we don't overhype the technology's capabilities. Conversely, the believers' enthusiasm reminds us of the transformative potential of AI. Ultimately, it's the bureaucrats who will play a pivotal role in shaping a future where AI flourishes within an ethical framework. Indeed, randomness in the business of life will continue to shape the destiny of AI. Just as nature throws unexpected curveballs, the unpredictable nature of human creativity, societal shifts, and unforeseen challenges will undoubtedly influence the course of AI development. It's within this dynamic interplay between human ingenuity and the evolving capabilities of AI that the true potential of this technology will be unlocked.

1. INTRODUCTION TO AI'S CREATIVE TENDENCIES

AI's Unexpected Creativity

Greetings. In the realm of artificial intelligence (AI), a captivating phenomenon emerges: AI's artistic side. Traditionally problem-solvers and data analysts, AI systems are now surprising us with outputs that transcend reality. This journey delves into the intriguing world of AI's imaginative capabilities.

Unveiling the Mystery

A fundamental question arises: how can AI, driven by algorithms and data, craft fictional narratives, images, and scenarios? We embark on a series of discussions to peel back the layers of this phenomenon.

At the heart of AI's creative spark lies a dance between data, algorithms, and human ingenuity. We explore how AI systems learn to identify patterns, extrapolate from existing knowledge, and synthesize novel creations. From generative models like Generative Adversarial Networks (GANs) to language models like GPT, each architecture offers a unique window into AI's creative process.

The exploration doesn't stop at observation. We contemplate the implications of AI's artistic endeavors. Ethical considerations around AI-generated content, including potential misinformation and the blurring of lines between human and machine-made art, demand examination.

Witnessing the Transformation

Through captivating stories and real-world examples, we witness the transformative power of AI's creative outputs across various domains, from entertainment and literature to healthcare and education. From AI-generated paintings to algorithmically crafted music, the possibilities are boundless and thought-provoking.

Navigating the Evolving Landscape

As we navigate the intricate landscape of AI-generated fiction, we confront both the awe-inspiring potential and the inherent risks of this technological evolution. With a critical eye and an open mind, we embark on a journey of discovery, inviting readers to join us in unraveling the mysteries of AI's creative tendencies and their profound implications for the future of human-machine interaction.

The Importance of Understanding AI's Creative Processes

In the rapidly evolving landscape of AI, understanding its creative processes is crucial. This delves beyond mere curiosity. Here, we elucidate the importance of gaining insight into AI's creative capabilities for various stakeholders, from researchers and developers to policymakers and the general public.

Fueling Innovation

Deciphering the algorithms and architectures behind AI's creative abilities fosters innovation and drives technological advancement. This understanding empowers researchers to push boundaries, leading to breakthroughs in art, design, and problem-solving.

Ethical Considerations

AI's creative outputs demand careful ethical examination. Questions of intellectual property rights and the societal impact of AI-generated content necessitate a nuanced understanding of AI's creative processes. This understanding is crucial for navigating ethical complexities and ensuring responsible AI development and deployment.

Enhancing User Experience

As AI integrates further into daily life, understanding its creative processes becomes vital for enhancing user experience and engagement. From personalized recommendations to immersive storytelling and interactive gameplay, AI-driven creativity shapes user interactions and drives satisfaction.

Transparency and Accountability

Shedding light on the inner workings of AI's creative processes is essential for building trust and accountability. Developers can provide users with insights into how AI-generated outputs are produced, empowering them to make informed decisions and hold AI systems accountable.

Education and Awareness

Educating the public about AI's creative capabilities is key to fostering digital literacy and promoting informed discourse. Demystifying AI's creative processes and dispelling misconceptions empowers individuals to engage thoughtfully with AI technologies, recognize their potential, and critically evaluate their societal, or (suicidal, whichever comes first) implications.

Cross-Disciplinary Collaboration

AI's creative processes intersect with various disciplines, including computer science, psychology, neuroscience, and the arts. Fostering collaboration across these fields allows us to leverage diverse insights, deepen our understanding of AI's creative abilities, and harness its potential for addressing complex challenges.

Empowering Human Creativity

Understanding AI's creative processes can empower, not replace, human creativity. Collaborating with AI systems as creative partners allows humans to augment their own creative endeavors, explore new avenues of expression, and unlock previously unimaginable possibilities.

Gaining insight into AI's creative processes is not a trivial pursuit; it's a critical imperative with far-reaching consequences. By embracing the complexities of AI's creative abilities with curiosity, skepticism, and ethical mindfulness, we can harness its transformative potential while safeguarding against potential risks and pitfalls.

2. ADVERSARIAL ATTACKS: DECEIVING THE MODEL

AI models, for all their advancements, face a critical hurdle: adversarial attacks. These malicious assaults disrupt a model's integrity, generating misleading outputs. Let's delve deeper into adversarial attacks and their impact on AI's reliability.

Crafted Deceptions

Adversarial attacks (AdvAttack) are meticulously crafted inputs designed to exploit weaknesses in AI. These attacks involve subtle alterations to input data, strategically engineered to deceive the model into making erroneous predictions. Imagine a stop sign – an adversarial attack might add a tiny, human-imperceptible sticker that tricks the AI into recognizing it as a speed limit sign.

The Ripple Effect of Deception

The core of an adversarial attack's power lies in its ability to introduce slight distortions in the input data. These distortions propagate through the model's layers, ultimately manifesting as misleading outputs. This can occur in image recognition, natural language processing, and various other AI applications, undermining the trustworthiness of AI systems.

Beyond the Technical Challenge

These attacks pose a significant challenge not just to the

technical aspects of AI but also to its ability to function effectively in real-world scenarios. Adversarial attacks raise broader societal concerns about AI's vulnerability to manipulation. From security systems compromised by adversarial examples to misinformation campaigns fueled by AI-generated content, these attacks threaten trust, privacy, and security in an increasingly AI-reliant world.

Fortifying the Defenses

Combating this threat necessitates a complex approach. We need robust model design, rigorous testing procedures, and continuous research into defense mechanisms.

Building Stronger Models

Designing AI models with intrinsic resilience to adversarial attacks is crucial. Researchers are exploring techniques like adversarial training, where models train on both clean and adversarially altered data to bolster their defenses.

Defense Through Adversity

Adversarial training involves incorporating adversarially crafted examples into the training data. By forcing the model to learn to defend against such attacks during training, this approach can enhance its robustness against adversarial perturbations.

The Art of Distillation

Defensive distillation is a technique where a model is trained to emulate the predictions of a larger, more robust model. This essentially involves creating a smaller, more efficient model that inherits the resilience of a larger one.

Hiding the Secrets

Techniques like gradient masking and input transformation aim to obscure the gradient information that attackers exploit to craft adversarial examples. Gradient masking disrupts the attacker's plan by hiding the gradient information used during training. This can involve randomizing these gradients or using a different set for real-world use compared to training. Essentially, the model learns in one way and operates in another, confusing attackers who rely on the training gradients.

Input transformation takes a different approach, altering the input data itself before feeding it to the model. Data augmentation, for example, creates slightly modified versions of the original data, making the model more robust to small perturbations that attackers might exploit. Normalization can also play a role, scaling the input data to make it less susceptible to manipulation.

These techniques offer a significant benefit: improved model resilience against adversarial attacks. This is especially critical in security-sensitive applications like facial recognition or autonomous vehicles, where a wrong decision can have severe consequences. However, there's always a trade-off – both techniques can introduce some overhead, potentially impacting the model's overall performance. Finding the right balance between obscuring information and maintaining accuracy is key to successful implementation.

Adding an Element of Chance

Introducing randomness into the model's architecture or training process can make it more resistant to adversarial attacks. Ensemble methods, which combine predictions from multiple models, can also improve robustness by reducing the impact of adversarial perturbations on individual models.

Randomization injects a layer of unpredictability into the model itself or its training process. This can involve techniques like random weights during initialization, dropout layers that randomly drop neurons during training, or even random noise added to the input data. By introducing this element of chance, attackers have a harder time figuring out the exact way to manipulate the model as the target keeps shifting slightly.

Ensemble methods take a different approach. Here, we train multiple independent models on the same data. When presented with a new input, each model makes its own prediction. The final output is then determined by aggregating the individual predictions, often through techniques like averaging or voting. This creates a more robust system – even if an attacker manages to fool one model with an adversarial example, the others are likely to remain unaffected, leading to a more accurate overall prediction.

The Fight Continues

Mitigating the impact of adversarial attacks on AI models necessitates the development of real-time detection and defense mechanisms. This includes methods for identifying adversarial examples during inference and adapting the model's behavior accordingly to minimize their influence.

Standardized Testing Grounds

Establishing standardized benchmarks and evaluation metrics for assessing an AI model's robustness against adversarial attacks is essential for progress in this field. These benchmarks provide researchers with a common platform for comparing various defense mechanisms and pinpointing areas for improvement.

The Future of AI Security

While adversarial attacks pose significant challenges, ongoing research and collaboration within the AI community are paving the way for innovative solutions to combat them effectively. By employing these multifaceted approaches, we can ensure that AI remains a trustworthy and reliable technology, safeguarding its potential to revolutionize various aspects of our lives.

In essence, adversarial attacks represent a critical hurdle on the path of AI development. However, by understanding their mechanisms and employing robust defense strategies, we can ensure the continued responsible and secure evolution of AI. As AI becomes increasingly integrated into our world, prioritizing its security and resilience against adversarial attacks is paramount. Through ongoing research, collaboration, and the development of effective defense mechanisms, we can harness the immense potential of AI while mitigating the risks associated with adversarial manipulation.

3. DATA CORRUPTION: WHEN REALITY TURNS UNRELIABLE

Types and Causes of Data Corruption in AI Systems

The Achilles' Heel of AI: Data Impurity

Artificial intelligence (AI) thrives on the veracity of its data. Just as flawed ingredients yield unreliable dishes, impure data begets unreliable AI outputs, eroding trust in these systems. Data impurity, encompassing various forms of inaccuracies and inconsistencies, presents a formidable challenge in the realm of AI.

A Spectrum of Impurities

One prevalent culprit is noise and distortion introduced during data acquisition, transmission, or storage. Picture a sensor malfunction during image capture, resulting in a garbled representation. Similarly, transmission errors can inject artifacts, while storage woes can lead to data loss or corruption.

Another threat arises from missing or incomplete data, often stemming from data collection errors or transmission/storage mishaps. Missing data creates gaps in the dataset, akin to an incomplete puzzle. When AI models are trained on fragmented information, the resulting models become unreliable.

Data can also be inherently biased or skewed. Bias surreptitiously creeps in when specific demographics or attributes are overrepresented or underrepresented. Imagine an AI system trained on facial recognition data skewed towards a particular race or gender. This bias can lead to prejudiced classifications. Skewness refers to the lopsided distribution of data across categories. For instance, an AI system trained on weather data from a perpetually sunny region might struggle with accurate predictions in a rain-drenched location.

Labeling errors occur when incorrect designations are assigned to data points. Envision a dataset where feline images are mistakenly labeled as canine. This mislabeling misleads AI models, leading to misinterpretations.

Data drift is a stealthy form of corruption. It occurs when the underlying data distribution surreptitiously changes over time. Think of an AI system trained on user preferences that encounters a sudden shift in those preferences due to a new trend. This data drift can render the AI model obsolete.

A particularly malicious form of data impurity is adversarial manipulation. Here, attackers deliberately introduce crafted inputs or perturbations to deceive AI systems. Imagine a self-driving car encountering a stop sign with a cleverly placed sticker that tricks the car's AI system into recognizing it as a yield sign.

Furthermore, data quality issues like inconsistencies, duplicates, outliers, and inaccuracies contribute to data impurity. Picture a dataset riddled with typos and contradictory information. This poor data quality jeopardizes the reliability of AI models trained on it, leading to misleading outputs.

Combating the Impure

Fortunately, we're not powerless against data impurity. By employing proactive measures like data cleaning, preprocessing, and validation techniques, we can significantly enhance the integrity and reliability of AI systems. Data cleaning involves identifying and rectifying errors, inconsistencies, and missing values. Preprocessing techniques like normalization and scaling can further refine the data for AI models. Finally, data validation involves rigorously testing the data to ensure its quality and suitability for the intended purpose.

Unquestionably, data impurity is a significant challenge in AI, demanding constant vigilance. By recognizing different forms of corruption and implementing robust data management practices, we can foster trust in AI systems and unlock their true potential to revolutionize various aspects of our lives. However, the fight against data corruption is an ongoing battle, requiring continuous research and development of new techniques to stay ahead of evolving threats.

IMPLICATIONS OF CORRUPTED DATA ON AI'S ABILITY TO GENERATE ACCURATE OUTPUTS

Flawed data poses a significant threat to the reliability of artificial intelligence (AI) systems. When trained on such data, AI models learn incorrect patterns, leading to inaccurate outputs and diminished performance. This has several critical implications:

Reduced Accuracy: AI models fed with corrupted data are prone to significant errors. Picture learning from a flawed textbook – the resulting knowledge will be unreliable. Similarly, AI models trained on bad data will produce inaccurate predictions and classifications.

Eroded Trust: We rely on AI for crucial tasks, from healthcare to finance. However, corrupted data undermines trust in AI outputs. If the foundation is shaky, so are the results. This can have serious consequences in critical domains.

Error Propagation: Corrupted data can cause errors to cascade through the AI system. Even if initially trained on clean data, encountering bad data during operation can lead to misleading outputs. This is particularly worrisome for safety-critical applications like autonomous vehicles.

Bias Amplification: Corrupted data can exacerbate existing biases in AI. Biases present in the data can be amplified by the model, leading to discriminatory outputs that unfairly impact specific groups.

Increased Vulnerability to Attacks: Corrupted data makes AI more susceptible to adversarial attacks (AdvAttack). Malicious actors can exploit these flaws to manipulate the model into incorrect predictions, further compromising reliability and posing security risks.

The real-world implications are stark. Corrupted data can render AI applications in fields like medical diagnosis, autonomous driving, and financial forecasting ineffective and even dangerous. Addressing this issue is crucial to ensure AI benefits society and minimizes potential harm.

4. BIAS AND SKEW: THE STORIES DATA TELL

Analyzing Bias and Skew in Training Data and Their Influence on AI's Output

In the realm of artificial intelligence, the stories told by data are not always impartial or balanced. Bias and skew in training data can significantly influence the outputs produced by AI systems, shaping the narratives they construct and the decisions they make.

When we talk about bias in training data, we're referring to the tendency for certain groups or attributes to be overrepresented or underrepresented, leading to distorted or inaccurate representations of reality. For example, if a facial recognition system is trained primarily on data consisting of lighter-skinned individuals, it may perform poorly when attempting to recognize darker-skinned faces due to the lack of diversity in the training data. Ask Google's Gemini.

Similarly, skewness in training data refers to the imbalance or uneven distribution of data across different classes or categories. This can occur when certain categories are disproportionately represented in the dataset, leading the AI system to prioritize or favor those categories over others. For instance, in a sentiment analysis model trained on customer reviews, an overrepresentation of positive reviews may skew the model's understanding of sentiment, leading to biased predictions.

Again, the influence of bias and skew in training data on AI's output cannot be overstated. AI systems learn from the patterns and associations present in the training data, and if the data is biased or skewed, the resulting outputs will reflect these biases and skewed perceptions of reality. This can have serious consequences, particularly in applications where fairness, equity, and impartiality are paramount.

For example, biased AI algorithms used in hiring processes may perpetuate discrimination against certain demographic groups, leading to unfair hiring practices. Similarly, skewed recommendations in online platforms may reinforce existing disparities and inequalities, exacerbating social divisions and marginalization.

Addressing bias and skew in training data requires a multifaceted approach that encompasses data collection, preprocessing, and algorithmic design. It's essential to ensure that training datasets are diverse, representative, and free from biases and skewness. Additionally, AI algorithms should be designed and evaluated with fairness and equity in mind, incorporating mechanisms to lessen bias and mitigate the influence of skewed data on the outputs.

Analyzing bias and skew in training data and understanding their influence on AI's output is a critical imperative, so that we can work towards building more equitable, inclusive, and trustworthy AI systems that reflect the diverse perspectives and experiences of the world around us.

STRATEGIES TO ADDRESS BIAS AND SKEW FOR MORE RELIABLE AI GENERATIONS

Addressing bias and skew in training data is essential for ensuring the reliability and fairness of AI-generated outputs.

One effective strategy is to prioritize diversity and inclusivity in data collection efforts. This helps to counteract biases that may arise from underrepresentation of certain groups and ensures that AI systems are trained on a more comprehensive and inclusive range of experiences.

Additionally, preprocessing techniques can be employed to mitigate bias and skewness in training data. For example, data augmentation methods such as oversampling or under sampling can help to balance class distributions and reduce skewness. Similarly, techniques like debiasing algorithms can be applied to identify and mitigate biases in the dataset, ensuring that AI models learn more impartial representations of the data.

Algorithmic design also plays a crucial role in addressing bias and skew. More work is needed. This includes considering the impact of AI decisions on different demographic groups and designing algorithms that minimize disparate treatment and outcomes.

Surely, transparency and accountability are essential for addressing bias and skew.. It's important to document and communicate the data sources, preprocessing steps, and algorithmic decisions involved in training AI models. This allows for greater scrutiny and oversight of the model's behavior, enabling stakeholders to identify and address potential biases or inaccuracies in the outputs.

Lastly, ongoing monitoring and evaluation are crucial for ensuring the effectiveness of bias and skew mitigation strategies.

Combating bias and data skew in training data demands a comprehensive strategy. This includes how we gather information, prepare it for analysis, design the algorithms themselves, ensure clarity in their decision-making, and continuously monitor them for fairness.

Ah, This Seems Complicated

You're absolutely right. Many solutions proposed to address bias and skew in AI systems can indeed appear academic and complex, making it challenging for data scientists to apply them effectively in real-life scenarios. Moreover, implementing these solutions can often involve substantial margins of error, further complicating the process.

One of the main challenges is the practical implementation of these strategies, which may require specialized expertise and resources that are not readily available to all data scientists. For example, preprocessing techniques such as data augmentation or debiasing algorithms can be technically demanding and computationally intensive, requiring significant time and effort to implement correctly.

Also, the effectiveness of these solutions can be difficult to assess and quantify, leading to uncertainty and ambiguity in their application. It's often unclear how much bias or skewness has been successfully mitigated, and there may be unintended consequences or trade-offs associated with the implementation of these strategies.

Moreover, the dynamic nature of data and AI systems introduces additional complexities and challenges. Data distributions may change over time, requiring continuous monitoring and adaptation of mitigation strategies. AI models may also exhibit unexpected behavior or vulnerabilities, necessitating ongoing evaluation and refinement of mitigation approaches.

In light of these challenges, it's essential for data scientists to tackle bias and skew mitigation with an open mind. Rather than expecting perfect solutions, it's important to acknowledge the inherent uncertainties and limitations associated with addressing bias and skew.

One approach is to adopt a "fail-fast" mentality, where experimentation and iteration are encouraged, and failures are viewed as opportunities for learning and improvement.

Collaboration and knowledge-sharing within the data science community can also play a crucial role in overcoming these challenges.

In brief, while addressing bias and skew can be daunting and error-prone, it's a good idea to approach the task with humility, pragmatism, and a willingness to experiment and learn from failure. Embracing uncertainty and collaborating with peers allows data scientists to navigate the complexities of bias and skew mitigation more effectively. This ultimately contributes to the development of more reliable and trustworthy AI systems.

5. DATA DRIFT: ADAPTING TO A CHANGING NARRATIVE

Recognizing Data Drift and Its Effects on AI's Interpretation of Reality

In the realm of artificial intelligence, data drift presents a significant challenge, requiring AI systems to adapt to a changing narrative.

Data drift refers to the phenomenon where the statistical properties of the data change over time, leading to discrepancies between the data used to train AI models and the data encountered during deployment. This can occur due to various factors, such as shifts in user behavior, changes in environmental conditions, or evolving trends and patterns in the underlying data.

AI systems learn from the patterns and associations present in the training data, and if the data distribution changes over time, the model's understanding of the underlying concepts may become outdated or incomplete. This can lead to inaccuracies, biases, and degraded performance in AI-generated outputs.

For example, consider a predictive maintenance system trained on historical sensor data from industrial machinery. If the operating conditions or maintenance practices change over time, the data collected in real-time may differ significantly from the data used to train the model. As a result, the predictive accuracy of the system may deteriorate, leading to increased maintenance costs or unexpected downtime.

Similarly, in applications such as financial forecasting or stock market prediction, data drift can have significant implications for decision-making. Changes in market dynamics, regulatory policies, or economic conditions can lead to shifts in the data distribution, affecting the reliability and validity of AI-generated predictions.

Recognizing and addressing data drift requires proactive monitoring and adaptation strategies. AI systems must continuously monitor incoming data streams for signs of drift and adjust their models accordingly. This may involve retraining the model with updated data, fine-tuning model parameters, or implementing adaptive learning algorithms that can dynamically adjust to changes in the data distribution.

It's important to establish robust validation and performance monitoring frameworks to evaluate the impact of data drift on AI-generated outputs. Organizations assess the reliability and accuracy of AI systems in real-world scenarios and identify potential drift-related issues through the process of tracking key performance metrics and comparing model predictions against ground truth data.

Indeed, recognizing data drift and its effects on AI's interpretation of reality is essential for building reliable and adaptive AI systems. Understanding the causes and consequences of data drift, alongside implementing proactive monitoring and adaptation strategies, allows organizations to ensure the accuracy, reliability, and relevance of AI-generated outputs within dynamic and evolving environments.

Techniques for Detecting and Responding to Data Drift in AI Systems

Data drift, the silent saboteur of AI systems, signifies a change in the distribution of data over time. This phenomenon can cripple the performance of models, leading to inaccurate predictions and unreliable outcomes. To combat this, we employ a multifaceted approach, using statistical measures and machine learning techniques to detect these shifts. One common method involves monitoring statistical properties of the data, such as mean, standard deviation, and distribution across various features. By comparing these properties over time, we can identify significant deviations that suggest data drift. For example, a sudden increase in the mean value of a particular feature could indicate a shift in the underlying data generating process. Visualization tools provide another powerful lens for examining data drift. Techniques like population stability index (PSI) and Kullback-Leibler (KL) divergence offer quantitative measures of the difference between data distributions. PSI helps assess shifts in the distribution of categorical features, while KL divergence measures the difference between probability distributions, providing insights into the extent of drift. Beyond statistical methods, machine learning models can be employed to detect anomalies or deviations from expected patterns. Techniques like Isolation Forest and One-Class SVM excel at identifying outliers, which can be indicative of data drift. Additionally, Autoencoders, when trained on the baseline data distribution, can reconstruct new data points. Significant reconstruction errors often point towards contamination, as the model struggles to accurately represent the shifted data.

Once contamination is detected, a prompt and appropriate response is crucial to maintain the integrity of the AI system. The specific response depends on the nature and severity of the drift, along with the impact on model performance. Retraining the model with the new data is often the most effective solution. The model, incorporating the shifted data distribution, can adapt and maintain its predictive accuracy. This may involve collecting a new dataset that reflects the current data distribution or using techniques like online learning to continuously update the model as new data arrives. In some cases, a simple model update may not suffice. If the underlying data generating process has fundamentally changed, a more comprehensive model redesign might be necessary. This could involve selecting different features, employing alternative algorithms, or even redefining the problem the model aims to solve. Data quality checks play a vital role in mitigating data drift. Implementing robust data validation and cleaning processes can help identify and rectify data errors or inconsistencies before they infiltrate the model. Additionally, establishing clear data governance protocols ensures data consistency and reduces the likelihood of unexpected shifts. Continuous monitoring remains essential even after addressing data drift. Establishing a system for tracking data distribution and model performance over time allows for early detection of future drifts and enables proactive intervention. This may involve setting up alerts for significant deviations in key metrics or implementing automated retraining processes when drift is detected. With a combination of detection techniques and response strategies, we can effectively mitigate the risks associated with contamination and ensure the ongoing accuracy and reliability of AI systems. As data landscapes continue to evolve, maintaining vigilance and adaptability will be key to navigating the dynamic world of artificial intelligence.

6. INTERPRETABILITY AND EXPLAIN ABILITY : UNVEILING THE BLACK BOX

The Importance of Interpretability and Explain ability in AI Systems

As AI technologies continue to permeate various aspects of our lives, from healthcare to finance to criminal justice, understanding how AI systems arrive at their decisions and predictions is essential for building trust, ensuring accountability, and addressing ethical concerns.

At its core, interpretability refers to the ability to understand and make sense of the internal workings of AI models. It involves unraveling the "black box" nature of complex algorithms to reveal the underlying logic, patterns, and features that drive their decision-making process. Explain ability , on the other hand, focuses on providing transparent and understandable explanations for the outputs generated by AI systems, allowing users to grasp the rationale behind the decisions made by the model.

The need for interpretability and explain ability arises from several critical considerations. First and foremost is the issue of trust. Users and stakeholders need to have confidence in artificial intelligence to make informed decisions based on their outputs. Without visibility into how AI models arrive at their conclusions, users may be reluctant to rely on AI-generated predictions, especially in high-stakes scenarios where the consequences of errors can be severe.

Interpretability and explain ability also play a crucial role in ensuring accountability and fairness. This is particularly important in domains where decisions made by AI systems can have significant social, economic, or legal implications, such as hiring, lending, or criminal justice.

Also, interpretability and explain ability are essential for fostering collaboration between humans and AI systems. In many real-world applications, AI technologies are used to augment human decision-making rather than replace it entirely. Interpretable models empower users to validate, critique, and refine AI-generated outputs, enabling a symbiotic relationship where human expertise complements AI capabilities.

To achieve interpretability and explain ability , various techniques and approaches can be employed. These include using simpler, more transparent models that are easier to interpret, such as decision trees or linear regression. Additionally, post-hoc explanation methods, such as feature importance analysis or model-agnostic techniques like LIME (Local Interpretable Model-Agnostic Explanations) and SHAP (SHapley Additive exPlanations), can provide insights into how individual predictions are influenced by input features.

In brief, interpretability and explain ability are essential pillars of trustworthy and responsible AI systems. It's vital to demystify the inner workings of AI models and provide transparent explanations for their decisions, so that we can build AI systems that are not only accurate and effective but also accountable, fair, and understandable to their users. As AI technologies continue to evolve and proliferate, ensuring interpretability and explain ability will be paramount in fostering trust and acceptance in AI-driven solutions.

Techniques for Interpreting and Explaining AI-Generated Outputs

The interpretation of AI-generated outputs play a crucial role in unveiling the black box of complex algorithms and providing transparent insights into how AI models arrive at their decisions.

One common technique for interpreting AI-generated outputs is feature importance analysis. This method identifies the most influential features or variables that contribute to a particular prediction or decision made by the model. By quantifying the impact of each feature on the model's output, users can gain insights into the underlying factors driving the model's behavior.

Another approach is model visualization, which involves representing the internal structure and decision-making process of AI models in a visually intuitive manner. Techniques such as decision trees, partial dependence plots, and activation maximization visualize how input features are processed and transformed by the model, allowing users to trace the flow of information and understand the model's decision logic.

Local interpretability methods provide explanations for individual predictions or instances generated by the AI model. Techniques like LIME (Local Interpretable Model-agnostic Explanations) and SHAP (S-Hapley Additive ex-Planations) generate interpretable explanations for specific data points by approximating the model's behavior in the vicinity of the instance of interest. These methods help users understand why the model made a particular prediction for a given input and identify potential biases or errors in the decision-making process.

Global interpretability techniques aim to provide a holistic understanding of the model's behavior across the entire dataset. Methods such as model inspection, sensitivity analysis, and feature importance ranking offer insights into how the model generalizes patterns and makes decisions across different subsets of data.

On top of that, natural language generation (NLG) techniques can be used to generate human-readable explanations or justifications for AI-generated outputs. By translating complex model predictions into plain language, NLG enables users to understand the reasoning behind the model's decisions in a more intuitive and accessible manner.

Incorporating these techniques into AI systems enhances their interpretability and explain ability , empowering users to trust, validate, and critique AI-generated outputs effectively.

Unveiling the Magic Behind Machine Decisions: Additive Explanations

Picture a complex machine making important choices, but you have no clue why it picks one option over another. This lack of transparency can be a problem for powerful tools like machine learning models. Additive explanations, also known as SHAP, aim to shed light on these decisions.

SHAP acts like a translator, deciphering the inner workings of a machine learning model. It breaks down a model's prediction into simple explanations, showing how each piece of information (like income in a loan approval decision) influences the final outcome.

For instance, if a model approves a loan, SHAP can reveal how much each factor, like income and credit score, contributed to that decision. This transparency builds trust – you understand why the model made that choice.

SHAP borrows a concept from economics called Shapley values to ensure fair explanations. Imagine a group project where everyone contributes, but how much credit should each person get? Shapley values make sure everyone gets a fair share of the credit based on their individual contribution. Similarly, SHAP ensures each piece of information gets credit for its role in the model's decision, even if it's connected to other factors.

Understanding the "Why": SHAP makes it easier to grasp how a model arrives at a decision, fostering trust and comfort in its use.

Identifying Key Players: SHAP helps pinpoint the most influential factors in a model's decision. This knowledge can be used to improve data quality or focus on the most impactful aspects.

Catching Hidden Biases: Unequal SHAP values for different groups might indicate bias in the model's training data. This allows for corrective action to ensure fairness.

Comparing the Choices: SHAP explanations can be used to compare different models, helping you choose the best one for a particular task.

While a powerful tool, SHAP has its limitations. It works well with various models, but for highly complex ones, the explanations might not be as detailed. Additionally, interpreting SHAP values might require some familiarity with data analysis concepts.

SHAP is a big step forward in making machine learning models more understandable. As these models become more intricate, tools like SHAP become even more crucial for responsible and ethical use.

Challenges And Limitations In Achieving Interpretability And Explain ability

Despite their importance for building trust, ensuring accountability, and fostering user acceptance, several obstacles hinder the effective interpretation and explanation of AI-generated outputs.

One significant challenge is the inherent complexity of modern AI models. Deep learning algorithms, in particular, often consist of numerous layers and millions of parameters, making them inherently opaque and difficult to interpret. The sheer size and complexity of these models pose challenges for traditional interpretation techniques, which may struggle to provide meaningful insights into the inner workings of the model.

Moreover, many AI models operate as "black boxes," meaning that they lack transparency in their decision-making process.

While these models may achieve high levels of accuracy and performance, their inscrutability raises concerns about the reliability and fairness of their outputs. Without visibility into how decisions are made, users may be reluctant to trust or rely on AI-generated predictions, especially in critical applications where errors can have significant consequences. And don't even dare to raise the output temperature!

Another challenge is the trade-off between accuracy and interpretability. In some cases, increasing the interpretability of an AI model may come at the cost of reducing its predictive performance. Simplifying the model or using interpretable algorithms may improve transparency but may also sacrifice predictive accuracy. Balancing these competing objectives is a complex task that requires careful consideration of the specific requirements and constraints of the application.

Besides, achieving interpretability and explain ability is often context-dependent and subjective. What constitutes a meaningful explanation may vary depending on the user's background, expertise, and expectations. Providing explanations that are both accurate and comprehensible to diverse audiences poses a significant challenge, as it requires tailoring the explanation to the user's level of understanding while preserving the essential insights into the model's decision-making process.

Ethical considerations also present challenges in achieving interpretability and explain ability . In some cases, revealing the inner workings of AI models may inadvertently disclose sensitive or confidential information, such as personally identifiable data or proprietary algorithms. Striking a balance between transparency and privacy is essential to ensure that users' rights and interests are protected while still providing meaningful insights into AI-generated outputs.

Finally, technical limitations and constraints may hinder the implementation of interpretable and explainable AI systems. Many existing techniques for interpretation and explanation are computationally intensive, requiring significant resources and time to execute. Real-time applications or resource-constrained environments may face challenges in deploying these techniques effectively.

Despite these challenges and limitations, efforts to achieve interpretability and explain ability continue to advance.

The Role of Interpretability in Building Trust and Transparency in AI Narratives

Interpretability refers to the ability to understand and make sense of the internal workings of AI models, while transparency involves providing clear and understandable explanations for the outputs generated by these models. Together, interpretability and transparency play a crucial role in fostering trust, accountability, and acceptance of AI systems among users and stakeholders.

One of the key ways interpretability enhances trust in AI narratives is by demystifying the black box of complex algorithms. Many AI models, particularly deep learning models, operate as opaque systems, making it challenging for users to understand how decisions are made.

Likewise, interpretability enables users to validate and verify the outputs produced by AI systems. When users understand the factors influencing the model's predictions or classifications, they can assess the model's accuracy, robustness, and fairness more effectively. This transparency empowers users to identify potential biases, errors, or inconsistencies in the AI-generated narratives and take appropriate corrective actions.

Interpretability also plays a critical role in promoting accountability and ethical behavior in the output. Yet again, when AI models operate as black boxes, it becomes challenging to assign responsibility for the decisions they make. Through transparent explanations of AI-generated outputs, interpretability allows stakeholders to hold AI systems accountable for their actions and outcomes. This accountability encourages developers and practitioners to adhere to ethical guidelines, regulations, and best practices in AI development and deployment.

Still, interpretability enhances the usability and adoption of AI systems by making them more understandable and accessible to users. In domains where AI technologies are used to augment human decision-making, such as healthcare or finance, interpretable models enable users to trust and rely on AI-generated recommendations with confidence. This trust facilitates the integration of AI technologies into existing workflows and decision-making processes, leading to broader acceptance and adoption.

With fewer shortcuts, prioritizing interpretability and transparency in AI development and deployment leads to more trustworthy, accountable, and user-centric AI systems. Such systems cater to the needs and expectations of users across diverse domains and applications.

7. CASE STUDIES AND EXAMPLES: STORIES FROM THE FRONTLINE OF AI FICTION

Real-world Instances of AI Generating Fictitious Outputs and Their Impacts

Exploring real-world instances of AI generating fictitious outputs offers valuable insights into the capabilities, limitations, and ethical implications. These case studies provide firsthand accounts of AI-generated narratives gone awry, shedding light on the challenges and opportunities in the evolving landscape of artificial intelligence.

One notable example is the infamous "deepfake" phenomenon, where AI technologies are used to create realistic but entirely fabricated images, videos, and audio recordings. Deepfake technology has been employed for various purposes, from celebrity impersonations to political misinformation campaigns. The proliferation of deepfake content poses significant challenges for media integrity, privacy rights, and public trust in digital media.

In the realm of natural language processing, AI-generated text has been used to generate fake news articles, spam emails, and fraudulent reviews. These deceptive narratives can spread misinformation, manipulate public opinion, and undermine trust in online content. Detecting and combating AI-generated text poses challenges for content moderation platforms, social media companies, and news organizations striving to maintain the integrity of their platforms.

AI-generated narratives have been leveraged for malicious purposes in cybersecurity attacks. For example, AI-powered phishing attacks can generate highly personalized and convincing messages to trick users into divulging sensitive information or clicking on malicious links. These sophisticated attacks exploit AI technologies to bypass traditional email filters and security measures, posing a significant threat to individuals and organizations alike.

In essence, real-world case studies of AI generating fictitious outputs highlight the multifaceted challenges and ethical dilemmas inherent in AI technologies. As AI technologies continue to evolve and proliferate, addressing these challenges will be paramount in ensuring the responsible and ethical development and deployment of AI systems.

When Data is Bad - Unveiling the Risks of Using Obsolete Information in Credit Ratings

The reliance of credit rating agencies on accurate and up-to-date data is crucial for providing reliable assessments of creditworthiness. However, concerns have been raised about the use of outdated and inaccurate data in the credit rating process. Let's explore the risks associated with this issue.

Agencies rely on a multitude of data sources to evaluate the financial health and credit risk of entities. These sources include financial statements, market data, economic indicators, and other relevant information. However, challenges arise when agencies use data that is outdated or contains inaccuracies, leading to potential imprecisions and misleading ratings. Several factors contribute to this problem:

Delayed Reporting: Financial statements and other financial data are typically released periodically, such as quarterly or annually. Delays in reporting can create a time gap between the release of information and the credit rating assessment. This time lag can be significant, especially in fast-paced and volatile markets, and may result in ratings that do not reflect the current financial condition of the entities.

Lagging Indicators: Some data used in credit rating analysis are considered lagging indicators, meaning they reflect past performance rather than current or future prospects. While historical data provides valuable insights into an entity's financial trajectory, relying solely on lagging indicators may fail to capture the evolving financial landscape and potential risks that could impact creditworthiness.

Data Quality and Integrity: The accuracy and integrity of the data used by credit evaluation companies are critical. Data sources may contain errors, omissions, or inconsistencies that can misrepresent the true financial position of entities. Inadequate data quality control mechanisms or limited access to reliable data sources can further exacerbate the risk of incorporating inaccurate information into credit ratings.

Limited Data Availability: Certain sectors or entities may have limited publicly available data, making it challenging for financial rating agencies to obtain comprehensive and reliable information. In such cases, agencies may have to rely on a limited dataset or extrapolate information, increasing the likelihood of potential inaccuracies and introducing additional uncertainties into the credit rating process.

Case Study: OUTDATED AND INACCURATE DATA - Unveiling the Risks of Using Obsolete Information in Credit Ratings

To illustrate the consequences of using outdated and

inaccurate data, let's consider a case study focusing on the credit rating industry. In this scenario, a credit rating agency relies on financial statements and market data from a company's previous fiscal year to assess its creditworthiness. However, due to delays in reporting and the lag in financial data availability, the agency's assessment does not reflect the company's current financial position.

As a result, investors and stakeholders may make decisions based on outdated information, leading to potential financial losses or missed opportunities. Moreover, the company's ability to access credit or secure favorable terms may be hindered by inaccurate credit ratings, impacting its growth and competitiveness in the market.

Fascinating or not, the use of outdated and inaccurate data in credit ratings poses significant risks to financial markets and stakeholders. Addressing these challenges requires greater transparency, data quality control mechanisms, and collaboration among industry participants to ensure the reliability and integrity of credit rating assessments.

More Bad Data - Unveiling the Pitfalls of Reliance on Economic Indicators

Economic indicators play a crucial role in shaping government policies, investment decisions, and public perception of a country's economic health. However, the accuracy and reliability of these indicators can be called into question, as illustrated by the following case study:

According to the weekly magazine "The Economist," as of March 2024, France and Italy, both G7 countries with a population of approximately 60 million, recorded a 7.5 percent unemployment rate. In contrast, in Southeast Asia, the Philippines, with a population of 109 million and heavily dependent on remittances, reported a surprisingly low unemployment rate of 4.5 percent.

This discrepancy raises eyebrows and prompts scrutiny of the reliability of economic indicators. Upon closer examination, it becomes evident that the reported unemployment rate in the Philippines may not accurately reflect the reality on the ground.

In the Philippines, there is no formal unemployment office, making it challenging to collect accurate data on unemployment rates. Moreover, the informal sector, which constitutes a significant portion of the economy, is often not captured in official statistics. As a result, the reported unemployment rate may not fully account for underemployment, disguised unemployment, or other factors affecting labor market participation.

Furthermore, the Philippines' heavy reliance on remittances from overseas Filipino workers may mask underlying economic vulnerabilities. A significant portion of the population works abroad, sending money back to their families in the archipelago. This inflow of remittances can artificially boost consumption and mask weaknesses in the domestic job market.

The persistence of unrealistically low unemployment rates in the Philippines, despite anecdotal evidence suggesting otherwise, highlights the limitations of relying solely on economic indicators. The disconnect between official statistics and lived experiences underscores the need for caution when interpreting and utilizing economic data for policymaking and decision-making purposes.

With fascination, the case of the Philippines' unemployment rate serves as a cautionary tale about the pitfalls of relying on economic indicators without considering their limitations and biases. Moving forward, greater transparency, data accuracy, and robust methodologies are needed to ensure the integrity and reliability of economic data, enabling more informed and effective decision-making processes.

Lessons Learned and Best Practices for Handling Fictitious Generations

Navigating the world of AI-generated narratives has taught us a lot. We've picked up some useful tips and tricks along the way to help us handle these fictional creations. These insights come from all sorts of experiences and can guide us in dealing with the risks linked to AI-generated stories.

One big lesson is that we need to be discerning. AI can craft narratives that seem super real, making it hard to tell fact from fiction. So, it's crucial for folks consuming AI-generated content to sharpen their critical thinking skills and learn to spot what's legit and what's not.

Another thing to watch out for is bias amplification. If AI models are trained on biased data, they can end up spreading and even beefing up societal biases. To avoid this, we've got to be picky about the data we use and keep an eye out for any biases that sneak into our models.

Then there's the importance of being upfront and honest. If you're using AI to create content, you've gotta be transparent about it. People deserve to know when AI's been involved in making something, so they can judge it for themselves.

Now, onto some best practices for dealing with AI-generated narratives:

First up, fact-checking is key. Before you put any AI-created content out there, make sure you've double-checked it for accuracy. That might mean getting a human to give it a once-over, comparing it to reliable sources, or using fact-checking tools.

Next, it's crucial to have some ethical guidelines in place. We need clear rules about how AI should be used to create narratives, covering everything from bias to transparency to accountability.

Education is also super important. We've gotta teach folks about AI-generated content and give them the skills to think critically about what they see online.

Plus, collaboration is key. We need to work together – researchers, developers, policymakers, and the public – to tackle the challenges that come with AI-generated narratives. Open dialogue helps us make sure we're developing this tech responsibly and ethically.

Ah! And don't forget about keeping an eye on things. We should regularly check our AI models for biases or unintended consequences and be ready to tweak them to make them better.

A couple more things to consider:

Remember that context matters. The impact of AI-generated stories can vary depending on where they're used. Entertainment might be one thing, but news or politics is a whole different ball game.

And finally, keep in mind that AI tech is always changing. We've gotta stay flexible and be ready to adapt our strategies as new challenges pop up.

8. FUTURE DIRECTIONS AND CHALLENGES: NAVIGATING THE UNCERTAIN TERRAIN OF AI CREATIVITY

Emerging Trends and Future Challenges in Understanding and Managing AI's Creative Tendencies

Looking ahead to the future of AI creativity, we find ourselves on a path filled with both promise and uncertainty. AI is poised to advance further, producing increasingly sophisticated and captivating narratives across various mediums like literature, visual arts, and music.

However, as AI's creative capabilities grow, so do the ethical considerations. We must grapple with questions of responsible use, ensuring that AI-generated content is wielded ethically and without bias. This raises concerns about privacy, ownership, and the implications of AI's creative output on society.

The future may see a shift towards collaboration between

humans and AI, where tools and platforms facilitate co-creation. This blending of human creativity with AI's capabilities could unlock new realms of possibility in artistic expression.

Yet, regulatory challenges loom on the horizon. Regulators must keep pace with AI innovation, establishing clear guidelines to govern its use in creative endeavors. Balancing innovation with ethical and societal concerns will be paramount.

As AI creativity permeates our cultural landscape, it will spark conversations about art, authorship, and the nature of creativity itself. These discussions will form our understanding of AI's role in shaping culture and society.

Despite the promise of AI creativity, technical limitations persist. Challenges such as bias, data scarcity, fantasy, and interpretability must be addressed to unlock AI's full potential. Continued research and innovation are essential to overcome these hurdles.

Likewise, ensuring accessibility and inclusivity in AI creativity is crucial. Efforts to democratize AI tools and promote diversity in development will help prevent further inequalities.

In navigating these future directions and challenges, collaboration, innovation, and a commitment to ethical AI development will be key. We must work harder, so that we can harness AI's creative potential to enrich our lives while mitigating risks and pitfalls.

However, it's important to note that the interest in AI is peaking, with many slowly turning away from using the technology on a daily basis. In light of this, we must ask ourselves: shall we bother to fix what's not working? This question prompts reflection on the societal impact of AI and the importance of addressing its limitations and challenges to ensure its continued relevance and utility.

Also, should AI lose the battle with copyright infringement, with the 'derivative work' wildcard in play, the technology will fade into oblivion. This underscores the critical importance of addressing legal and ethical concerns surrounding AI-generated content to ensure its sustainability and longevity in the creative landscape.

What If

Let's explore some intriguing "what if" scenarios about the future of AI creativity. These questions are like little thought experiments that can spark some interesting discussions. We'll ponder hypothetical situations, consider potential challenges, and think about the ethical implications of where AI might lead us.

Let's start with the idea of AI superintelligence. Picture if AI became super smart, like, way smarter than humans. What would that mean for us? It's a bit like something out of a sci-fi movie, but it's also a serious topic that makes us think about our place in the world and what it means to be intelligent.

Then there's the question of creativity without limits. What if AI could churn out masterpieces of art, music, and literature with ease? It's an exciting thought, but it also raises questions about the role of humans in the creative process. Are we still the artists, or are we just along for the ride?

Next up is the idea of the singularity. This is the concept that AI could advance so quickly that it surpasses human intelligence in the blink of an eye. What would a world dominated by super-smart machines look like? Would it be a utopia or a dystopia? It's a big question that forces us to consider the implications of rapid technological progress.

Then there's the ethical dilemmas that AI might face. Can machines have morals? And if they can, who decides what's right and wrong? It's a tricky question that makes us think about the relationship between humans and AI and what it means to be ethical in a world run by machines.

Of course, sometimes things don't go as planned. What if AI development led to unexpected consequences? It's a scary thought, but it's also a reminder that we need to be careful with this technology and think about the long-term impacts.

But it's not all doom and gloom. What if humans and AI could team up to solve problems and create cool stuff together? It's an idea that's not so far-fetched. We're already seeing AI helping out in all sorts of fields, from science to art to everyday tasks.

And finally, let's talk about the future of work. What if AI took over a bunch of our jobs? It's a real concern, especially with all the talk about automation. But it's also an opportunity to rethink how we work and what we value as a society.

These "what if" scenarios might seem like something out of a sci-fi novel, but they're also important to think about. They make us question our assumptions, consider different possibilities, and prepare for whatever the future might hold. So let's dive in and see where our imaginations take us!

9. CONCLUSION: EMBRACING THE QUANTUM CONSCIOUSNESS WITH MIND TRAINING LIKE AI

It's intriguing to consider this conversation in the context of quantum consciousness (or a brief explanation of the Quantum Self). As explored in my other work ("MIND TRAINING LIKE AI"), our exploration of consciousness can be a profound journey into the nature of reality and the essence of the self. We might uncover insights by drawing parallels between the transformative power of mind training and the adaptive capabilities of AI algorithms.

Reflecting on this voyage, it becomes clear that the observer shapes reality. We are not mere spectators but active participants in the web of existence. Our consciousness influences our experiences and the world around us, echoing the themes of interconnectedness and co-creation explored in the power of AI.

Yet, amidst the marvels of AI technology, we must remember that it should not serve as a desperate solution to a lack of creativity or a shortcut to cognitive prowess. While AI can offer valuable insights and assistance, true growth and understanding come from within. Mind training, like AI, allows us to adapt and evolve, unlocking latent potentials and expanding our consciousness. By nurturing our inner resources, we cultivate resilience, creativity, and well-being.

In a world increasingly reliant on AI and other technologies, training our minds becomes crucial. It offers a path to becoming less dependent on external systems and toxic technologies. By embracing quantum physics and mind training, we embark on a journey of self-discovery that leads to a more enriched and awakened existence.

This journey is not isolated but interconnected with broader themes explored throughout our exploration. From the implications of AI superintelligence to the ethical considerations of AI development, each chapter has contributed to our understanding of the complex interplay between technology and consciousness.

As we navigate the uncertain terrain of AI creativity and the quantum self, let us remain mindful of the interconnectedness of all things and the transformative power of mind training. Together, we can shape a reality that reflects our highest ideals and contributes to the well-being of all beings.

Thank you for joining us on this journey of exploration and discovery.

KEY FINDINGS AND INSIGHTS

1. AdvAttack pose significant challenges to AI systems, highlighting the importance of robustness and security measures to safeguard against deceptive inputs.

2. Data drift can adversely impact the performance of AI models over time, emphasizing the need for continuous monitoring and adaptation to changing data distributions.

3. Bias and skew in training data can lead to biased outputs from AI models, underscoring the importance of addressing biases and ensuring fairness in AI development.

4. Interpretability and explain ability are essential for understanding AI decisions and promoting trust, transparency, and accountability in AI.

5. Ethical considerations play a critical role in AI development and deployment, guiding responsible and ethical use of AI technology to mitigate potential risks and harms.

6. Mind training practices offer a complementary approach to AI technology, empowering individuals to enhance mental well-being, cognitive function, and self-awareness.

A+ CONTENT FROM 'MIND TRAINING LIKE AI'

Embarking on a voyage of self-discovery and growth with Mind Training Like AI

As we contemplate the profound implications of artificial intelligence and its societal impact, we find intriguing parallels between AI's evolution and the potential for human transformation through mind training. Just as AI algorithms adapt and refine through continuous learning, we too can harness mind training to nurture heightened self-awareness, resilience, and empathy.

In this era of pervasive technology, where digital advancements shape our daily lives, the imperative to cultivate inner wisdom and emotional intelligence becomes increasingly evident. Practices such as meditation, mindfulness, and introspection furnish invaluable resources for navigating life's complexities with clarity and composure.

Through consistent mind training, we embark on a journey of self-exploration, delving into the depths of our consciousness and unraveling the enigmas of our minds. By scrutinizing our thoughts, emotions, and behaviors, we acquire profound insights, liberating ourselves from restrictive patterns and fostering mental agility and emotional fortitude.

In a manner akin to AI algorithms refining their models based on feedback and experience, we refine our mental frameworks through deliberate effort and dedication. By nurturing qualities like mindfulness, empathy, and compassion, we expand our capacity for connection and understanding, fostering richer, more authentic relationships.

Moreover, as we engage in mind training resembling AI's adaptive nature, we unlock latent potentials and faculties dormant within us, accessing boundless creativity and wisdom. Through cultivating presence and awareness, we traverse our inner landscapes with grace and poise, embracing life's vicissitudes as catalysts for growth and enlightenment.

The journey of self-discovery and transformation is devoid of shortcuts or facile solutions; it demands steadfast commitment, resilience, and an appetite for the unknown. Yet, just as AI algorithms continually stretch the boundaries of possibility, so too can we transcend perceived limitations and actualize our innate potential.

As we navigate the uncharted terrain of the future, let us embark on this transformative odyssey with open hearts and curious minds. Let us harness the power of mind training to cultivate greater insight, empathy, and resilience, and to chart a course towards a more enlightened and compassionate society.

In the spirit of perpetual evolution and discovery, may we approach the journey ahead with courage and conviction, recognizing that the true essence of adventure lies not in the destination, but in the profound transformations that unfold along the way.

GLOSSARY

1. Artificial Intelligence (AI): A branch of computer science that focuses on creating systems capable of performing tasks that typically require human intelligence, such as learning, problem-solving, and decision-making.

2. Adversarial Attacks or AdvAttack: Techniques aimed at deceiving AI models by feeding them manipulated or crafted input data to produce incorrect outputs.

3. Data Drift: The phenomenon where the statistical properties of a dataset change over time, leading to shifts in the performance of AI models trained on that data.

4. Bias and Skew: Systematic errors or distortions in data that can lead to biased or skewed outputs from AI models.

5. Interpretablity and Explain ability : The ability to understand and interpret the decisions made by AI models, as well as the underlying factors that contribute to those decisions.

6. Quantum Self: The concept that explores the relationship between consciousness and quantum physics, suggesting that consciousness may be influenced by quantum phenomena.

7. Mind Training: Practices and techniques aimed at improving mental well-being, cognitive function, and self-awareness, such as meditation, mindfulness, and contemplation.

8. Singularity: A hypothetical future event where AI and technology advance to the point where they surpass human

intelligence, leading to rapid and unpredictable societal change.

9. Superintelligence: An AI system that possesses intelligence surpassing that of the brightest and most gifted human minds across all domains of knowledge and skill.

10. Ethical Dilemmas: Complex moral issues and quandaries arising from the development and deployment of AI technology, such as privacy concerns, bias, and accountability.

11. Cognitive Prowess: The capacity for advanced cognitive abilities, such as reasoning, problem-solving, and creativity.

12. Toxic Technologies: Technologies or systems that have negative impacts on individuals, society, or the environment, often due to misuse, exploitation, or unintended consequences.

Q&A

Here are some questions and answers based on the topics we've discussed:

Q: What are some common types of AdvAttack against AI systems?
A: AdvAttack can take various forms, including adding imperceptible noise to images to fool image recognition systems, manipulating input data to generate incorrect predictions, and exploiting vulnerabilities in machine learning algorithms to deceive models.

Q: How does data drift impact the performance of AI models?
A: Data drift can significantly affect the performance of AI models by causing shifts in the statistical properties of the data they were trained on. This can lead to deteriorating accuracy and reliability over time, as the models may struggle to adapt to changes in the data distribution.

Q: Why is interpretability and explain ability important in AI?
A: Interpretability and explain ability are crucial for understanding how AI models make decisions and for identifying potential biases or errors. They enable users to trust and verify the outputs of AI systems, promote accountability and transparency, and facilitate collaboration between humans and machines.

Q: What are some ethical considerations surrounding AI development and deployment?
A: Ethical considerations in AI include issues such as privacy,

fairness, accountability, transparency, and the potential societal impacts of AI technology. Ensuring that AI systems are developed and used responsibly requires addressing these concerns and implementing ethical guidelines and frameworks.

Q: How can mind training help mitigate reliance on AI and other technologies?

A: Mind training practices such as meditation, mindfulness, and contemplation can enhance mental well-being, cognitive function, and self-awareness. By cultivating inner resources and resilience, individuals can become less dependent on external technologies and develop a deeper understanding of themselves and the world around them.

SUGGESTED READINGS

1. "Adversarial Machine Learning" by Battista Biggio and Fabio Roli - This book provides a comprehensive overview of AdvAttack and defenses in machine learning, offering insights into the latest techniques and strategies for securing AI systems.

2. "Data Science for Business: What You Need to Know about Data Mining and Data-Analytic Thinking" by Foster Provost and Tom Fawcett - This book offers practical guidance on leveraging data science and machine learning techniques for business applications, with a focus on ethical considerations and real-world case studies.

3. "Interpretable Machine Learning" by Christoph Molnar - This book explores methods and techniques for interpreting and explaining machine learning models, providing practical tools and insights for understanding AI decisions and fostering trust and transparency.

4. "Ethics of Artificial Intelligence and Robotics" edited by Vincent C. Müller and Nick Bostrom - This collection of essays examines the ethical implications of AI and robotics, covering topics such as fairness, accountability, transparency, and the societal impacts of AI technology.

5. "The Mind Illuminated: A Complete Meditation Guide Integrating Buddhist Wisdom and Brain Science" by Culadasa

(John Yates) - This comprehensive meditation guide combines traditional Buddhist teachings with modern neuroscience research, offering practical techniques for cultivating mindfulness, concentration, and insight.

6. "How to Create a Mind: The Secret of Human Thought Revealed" by Ray Kurzweil - In this book, futurist Ray Kurzweil explores the nature of intelligence and consciousness, drawing parallels between the workings of the human brain and artificial intelligence.

7. "The Age of Spiritual Machines: When Computers Exceed Human Intelligence" by Ray Kurzweil - Another book by Ray Kurzweil, this work delves into the future implications of AI and technology, envisioning a world where machines surpass human intelligence and exploring the ethical and societal implications of such advancements.

These readings offer valuable insights and perspectives on the topics discussed, providing a deeper understanding of AI, ethics, consciousness, and the intersection of technology and humanity. Reading is good.

ABOUT THE AUTHOR

Alfonso Borello

Alfonso Borello approaches writing with dignity, humility, and empathy, prioritizing personal satisfaction over external recognition. While occasionally sharing his work, he expects little and finds reward in cognitive exercise, spiritual growth, and personal transformation. His writing reflects authenticity and empathy, aiming to connect with readers on a deeper level.

BOOKS BY THIS AUTHOR

Mind Training Like Ai

Imagine a world where minds are sculpted like AI: each individual undergoing a transformative process akin to neural network training. Here, the concept of "mind training like AI" takes center stage—a provocative notion challenging traditional views of learning and self-improvement. Picture human minds as dynamic entities, continuously evolving and adapting, shaped by the principles of artificial intelligence.

In this realm, the boundaries between human cognition and machine learning blur, ushering in a new era of cognitive enhancement. Layers of knowledge, experiences, and insights intertwine to form a dynamic network of cognitive pathways. Minds become fluid, adaptive entities, responding to stimuli and feedback in real-time, much like the algorithms of AI.

This work invites you to envision a future where the synergy between human intelligence and machine learning knows no bounds. It challenges conventional notions of human potential, offering a glimpse into the transformative power of mind training like AI. As we explore this concept further, we unlock the secrets of human cognition and chart a course towards unprecedented levels of intelligence and self-discovery.

Excellence Won't Save You

In a world obsessed with the pursuit of excellence, where success is often equated with perfection, it's time to challenge the status quo. "Excellence Won't Save You" invites readers on a thought-provoking journey through the complexities of achievement and the pitfalls of conventional wisdom.

Delving into the depths of history, philosophy, and human psychology, this book unravels the illusions of success that have long captivated our collective consciousness. From the fallacy of reasoning by analogy to the dangers of social media-driven expectations, it sheds light on the myths and misconceptions that surround the pursuit of excellence.

Drawing on real-life examples, captivating narratives, and insightful analysis, "Excellence Won't Save You" offers a fresh perspective on what it truly means to thrive in a world that often values appearances over authenticity. It challenges readers to question their assumptions, embrace uncertainty, and redefine their notions of success.

You'll discover:

The fallacy of reasoning by analogy: Why past achievements don't guarantee future success.
The paradox of excellence: How the relentless pursuit of perfection can lead to disillusionment and burnout.
The importance of authenticity: Why embracing your flaws and vulnerabilities is essential for true fulfillment.
Strategies for resilience: How to navigate failure, setbacks, and uncertainty with grace and resilience.
Redefining success: Why success is more than just external validation or societal expectations.

Whether you're a seasoned leader, a budding entrepreneur, or simply someone searching for meaning in a chaotic world, this book provides a roadmap for navigating the complexities of achievement with clarity and purpose. It's a reminder that true excellence isn't found in perfection, but in the courage to embrace our imperfections and pursue a path that is uniquely our own.

"Excellence Won't Save You" is not just another self-help book—it's a manifesto for those who dare to challenge the status quo, defy the odds, and chart their own course towards a life of meaning and fulfillment. It's time to break free from the illusions of success and discover what truly matters in the pursuit of excellence.

Quantum Consciousness: How The Principles Of Quantum Mechanics Explain The Mysteries Of Human Experience

In "Quantum Consciousness: How the Principles of Quantum Mechanics Explain the Mysteries of Human Experience," readers are taken on a journey to explore the exciting and controversial field of quantum consciousness. This book introduces the fundamental principles of quantum mechanics and explores how they may help explain the enigmatic nature of human consciousness.

Through a combination of scientific research, philosophical inquiry, and personal anecdotes, the author examines the potential implications of a quantum model of consciousness on our understanding of the universe, the mind-body problem, free will, spirituality, and more. This book is an essential read for anyone interested in the intersection of science, philosophy, and spirituality, and the exciting possibilities that arise when these disciplines are brought together.

The Ecology Of The Mind: Exploring The Relationship Between Inner And Outer Worlds

Introducing a captivating journey through the intricate webs of human and ecological systems - this book invites you to explore the fascinating interplay between the inner and outer worlds. As you delve into the concepts of systems thinking, ecological perception, embodied cognition, and regenerative transformation, you will discover a new way of seeing the world, one that honors the complexity and diversity of all life forms.

Drawing on the pioneering ideas of Gregory Bateson, the author takes you on a captivating journey that traverses the fields of ecology, psychology, philosophy, and ethics. From the intricate dynamics of communication and the double bind to the intricate patterns of cultural evolution, this book illuminates the complex relationships that shape our world.

The Ecology of the Mind is a reminder that we are not separate from nature but part of it, and that our choices have the power to shape the future of our planet. Whether you are a student of ecology or a concerned citizen, this book will inspire you to think differently, act boldly, and embrace the complexity of the world we inhabit.

www.ingramcontent.com/pod-product-compliance
Lightning Source LLC
LaVergne TN
LVHW010040070326
832903LV00071B/4468
9798323254347